WAITING HERE FOR YOU

AN ADVENT JOURNEY OF HOPE

—

LOUIE GIGLIO

passionpublishing

atlanta, georgia

BUT AS FOR ME,

I WILL WATCH EXPECTANTLY

FOR THE LORD...

(MICAH 7:7, NASB)

WHAT ARE YOU WAITING FOR?

Welcome to the season of Advent, a celebration that traditionally spans the four Sundays leading up to Christmas. And, welcome to *Waiting Here for You*, a devotional guide filled with hope for everyone who is waiting for something or someone. Whether you are waiting on a resolution, a diagnosis, a relationship, a breakthrough, or a rescue, God has a message of hope for you.

Advent simply means arrival—in the case of Christmas we celebrate the arrival of Jesus, the greatest gift ever given to the world. For on a chaotic night in the little town of Bethlehem a miracle happened. Down the slope of a hill, in a cave carved out by the wind and rain, a place where animals took shelter in the storm, a Savior was born who would take away the sins of the world.

But Jesus didn't arrive without a wait. While you and I simply turn the page, moving effortlessly from the end of the Old Testament promises to the opening of Matthew's Gospel, it wasn't quite that easy. Four hundred years of silence spanned the gap between the final prophecies spoken in Malachi (the last Old Testament book) and the birth of Christ.

Imagine four hundred years without any recorded word from God—no voice, no prophet, nothing. Imagine the agony of waiting, and the struggle to keep faith in the promises given long before. You can almost hear the questions being passed from one generation to the next. Had God vanished? Was He ever really there? Was faith in Him just a waste?

Suddenly, when the time was right, Bethlehem's fields lit up like noonday as angels proclaimed, *Glory to God in the highest, and on earth peace among men on whom his favor rests*.

The wait was over. The silence was broken. Heaven unleashed thunderous applause. And in a feeding trough, Jesus was born. God in human flesh! The Son of God had become the Son of Man. Emmanuel—God with us!

Christmas is a story of longing fulfilled. That's why it gives us reason to celebrate the goodness and nearness of God in the midst of our waiting seasons. As we struggle with our own sense of silence, and as we strain to see God at work in our convoluted lives, Christmas urges us on by reminding us that God will come through on His promises.

Sadly, the frenzy we call the *holiday season* is a mad dash of tinsel and toys, driven more by consumerism than anything else. Ironically, the season that marks the arrival of the Prince of Peace has somehow begun to leave us feeling frantic, stressed, alone and peace-*less*. If we're not careful, the season can create a perfect storm of anxiety that will cause us to miss God's voice.

But, it doesn't have to be this way. If we ask Him, God will give us the grace to slow the pace. And He will help us remember how loved we are and how trustworthy He is. If we wait expectantly for Him, God will lift our eyes and draw near to us. He will remind us that waiting is not wasting when we are waiting on His plans to unfold. He will anchor our hearts in the bedrock of His faithfulness.

My prayer is that this Advent devotion will encourage and fortify your faith so, ultimately, hope may bloom again.

Each day throughout this Advent journey you will find Scripture readings, Christian meditations, words of encouragement, and prayers to help you re-center your thoughts and confidence in God's purposes for your life.

Louie Giglio

I encourage you to carve out a few moments daily to embrace God's faithfulness through reflection, worship, and prayer. As you do, there's a good chance something new will be born in your heart…and when Christmas day arrives you will be able to truly celebrate what God has done and what He promises to do.

So let's get started. What are you waiting for?

THE STORY OF CHRISTMAS GRACE

This wasn't how Aaron planned on spending Christmas. He glanced around the room at the tilting artificial tree in the corner, its pathetic single strand of twinkling lights reflecting off the wall. On a nearby table, a plastic platter hosted a collection of stale cookies, each shaped like an angel. But no amount of Christmas cheer could brighten the mood or bring comfort to the uneasy few scattered around the room. Unlike other happy Christmas destinations, no one was there by choice. Like Aaron's family, they all had been summoned by circumstances beyond their control.

It had been weeks since Aaron had first found the room tucked at the end of a third floor hall-way. By now he could navigate the walk in his sleep. Circle into the south deck, traverse the long hallway from building B, take the north elevators to the third floor, two right turns and another hallway to what seemed like a holding cell of hope. By now the minutes were dragging into hours and the hours into days. Outside, the sky faded from day to night to day so many times he had lost count. Sometimes he stayed all day, other times all night. And when exhaustion finally drew him into restless sleep, he would awaken with the fleeting possibility that this was all a crazy dream. And then he'd unfold the small piece of paper in his pocket and read his mom's handwritten note.

We'll be okay. Love you.

Aaron had figured out how the system worked. He knew his best chance to get an update on his mom's condition was to be in the little hallway between the ICU waiting room and the entrance to the patient area around 7:00 a.m. Fortunately, that morning Dr. Amer rounded the corner on cue. Their eyes met and the doctor crossed the hall with determination.

"Is your family here with you?" he said.

"No, it's just me this morning," Aaron said. "Is everything okay?"

Aaron knew the answer before he asked the question. He'd known the answer to that question since his dad passed away. The sudden loss and unrelenting grief made for three long, miserable years, and just when the pain was beginning to fade his mom was diagnosed with cancer.

She fought heroically through the first round of treatments and miraculously came back from the brink of death. The fight was fierce, but her faith was unshaken. Cancer roared, but she roared back, buoyed by a confidence in God that was like bedrock. Lying on her hospital bed, nauseous from chemo, plugged into what seemed like a dozen machines, she would say, "Jesus beat death and so will I."

When Aaron wrestled with her illness and questioned God's goodness, she always found a way to reassure him. Even when she was exhausted and unable to speak she would leave handwritten notes waiting by her bedside.

Just resting. Don't worry. Love, Mom.

It's going to be okay. Love, Mom.

But this time it was harder to be optimistic. The cancer was back with a vengeance. The treatments that once saved her life were proving ineffective. Complications were creeping in from every angle and each one seemed to open the door to a whole new set of challenges. The specialists at St. Luke's were running out of options. She had been in the hospital this time since the day before Thanksgiving, and on more than one occasion it looked like the end had come. Her unstable condition made it difficult to leave her side, but the days turned into weeks and the demands of life outside the waiting room walls made not leaving impossible. Somehow in the blur, Christmas had come and Aaron's family was learning the hard way that cancer doesn't care what day it is.

Matt, Aaron's older brother, had flown home to Chicago to be with his wife and their three small children for Christmas morning. Juggling his desire to be near his mom, combined with his job as a commodity trader was bringing him to the breaking point. Matt was scheduled to return in two days. Anna, Aaron's little sister, made the hour-long drive home the previous night to get some much needed sleep. Last week she and her husband Garrett were informed that their long-awaited adoption was finally going through—at least that's what they were hoping for.

Anna and Garrett had spent five grueling years on a merry-go-round of disappointment. Once, their hearts were set on a little girl only to have the birth mom change her mind at the very last minute. Another time the courts intervened. Earlier in the year they actually held their new baby boy, but just before the allotted time expired the father decided not to sign the adoption papers.

In the fall they switched to a local agency that placed babies born to moms addicted to drugs and alcohol, and were told to be ready by mid-January. So, with Anna's mom clinging to life, they were once again in the prep mode, doing what it seemed they perpetually found themselves doing—waiting for a baby to come.

In the hallway it was just Aaron and Dr. Amer.

"She asked for you," Dr. Amer said. "She asked if the three of you were here."

"She spoke?"

"Yes."

"Seriously?"

Dr. Amer nodded with a surprised look on his face.

Aaron rushed passed Dr. Amer and pushed through the doors to the ICU patient area. His mom had hardly been awake in the past seventy-two hours, let alone conscious enough to speak. Breaking protocol, he hurried passed the nurse's station without calling to see if a visit was allowed. He reached room number seven and stepped inside.

She was lying in her bed with her face turned away from the door. The blinds were open, but the morning light fell flat into the room. Could she really be awake and alert? Aaron crept up to her bedside without making a sound.

"Mom?"

to be continued...

GOD WORKS WHILE WE WAIT.

JUST THE RIGHT TIME

Galatians 4:4–5 (ESV)

But when the fullness of time had come, God sent forth his Son, born of woman, born under the law, to redeem those who were under the law, so that we might receive adoption as sons (and daughters)*.

*(added by author)

REFLECTION

While God rarely comes at *our* appointed time, He always comes at the *right* time. A Savior had been promised to God's people for centuries. And for centuries they longed and prayed for rescue to no avail. Yet on the right day, in the right place, at the right time, Jesus was born. Christmas reminds us that God comes through on His promise.

We are all waiting on something or someone, often wondering if God has forgotten us. Is that where you are today? In your waiting, let the birth of Christ encourage you. Just because God hasn't come through (as far as you can see), it doesn't mean He has abandoned you. This very minute He's working for His glory and for your good. Though circumstances say otherwise, God is moving right now to fulfill His long-appointed plans for you. Don't give up. Take hope in the manger and know that you are prized by Jesus. He stepped down from heaven for you. And just as He loved you that day, He loves you right now. And Jesus is with you, even in the storm.

MEDITATION
Hark the Glad Sound

Hark the glad sound! The Savior comes,
The Savior promised long;
Let ev'ry heart prepare a throne,
And ev'ry voice a song.

He comes the pris'ners to release,
In Satan's bondage held.
The gates of brass before Him burst,
The iron fetters yield.

He comes the broken heart to bind,
The bleeding soul to cure,
And with the treasures of His grace
To enrich the humble poor.

Our glad hosannas, Prince of Peace,
Thy welcome shall proclaim,
And heav'ns eternal arches ring
With Thy beloved name.

Philip Doddridge, 1702–1751

PRAYER

Father, meet me in the waiting, the place where I long for what is not fully in view. Still my heart and give me the ability to know that You are near. I believe Your plans are good. I see it in the birth of Your only Son. But sometimes I struggle to see beyond the haze that surrounds me. Renew my confidence as I lift my eyes to You. Be glorified in my life during this season of expectation. Amen.

GOD WORKS WHILE WE WAIT

Lamentations 3:26 (NIV)

It is good to wait quietly for the salvation of the LORD.

REFLECTION

If we are honest, we all hate to wait. In fact, most often we say something like, "I can't believe this is taking so long; it's costing me time I don't have!" That's because most of us consider *waiting* to be *wasting*. But it's not so with our God.

God works while we wait. Even when you can't see what He is doing, God is always orchestrating the events of heaven and earth to accomplish His purposes for your life. Trust in His unfailing love—love that moved Him to send a Savior from heaven to restore and rescue you. God's plans for your life will not be thwarted. Wait patiently, knowing that *waiting is never wasted when you are waiting on God.*

MEDITATION
Come Thou Long Expected Jesus

Come, Thou long expected Jesus
Born to set Thy people free;
From our fears and sins release us,
Let us find our rest in Thee
Israel's Strength and Consolation,
Hope of all the earth Thou art;
Dear Desire of every nation,
Joy of every longing heart.

Born Thy people to deliver,
Born a child and yet a King,
Born to reign in us forever,
Now Thy gracious kingdom bring.
By Thine own eternal Spirit
Rule in all our hearts alone;
By Thine all sufficient merit,
Raise us to Thy glorious throne.

Charles Wesley, 1707–1788

PRAYER

Father, I am here waiting for You. My heart and hands are open to Your purposes and plans for my life. Give me the patience I so desperately need and lead me in my waiting. Though my feelings may not be there just yet, I believe You are moving on my behalf right this minute, protecting, defending, preparing, providing. Give me grace to keep trusting in You in the face of the gale force winds of doubt that are blowing all around me. Anchor my heart in You. Amen.

CHOOSE GOD'S WAY

Isaiah 30:15b,18b (NIV)

In repentance and rest is your salvation, in quietness and trust is your strength, but you would have none of it. Yet the Lord LONGS TO BE GRACIOUS TO YOU; therefore he will rise up to show you compassion. For the Lord IS A GOD OF JUSTICE. Blessed are all who wait for him!

REFLECTION

It's easy to bail on God at the first sign of trouble. We fret, we worry, we make new plans, we settle for shortcuts. We take matters into our own hands and soon feel the weight of anxiety and worry. But there is another way—the quiet way of rest and trust. God is sovereign (He runs the world) and He is in control. During this Advent journey, keep making the confident decision to choose God's way. Guard your heart from any voice that offers a "quick fix." Instead, say, "Jesus, I will wait on You."

The best things in life take time, and the payoff of doing things God's way is always better. But the enemy is crafty and determined to deceive us, trying to convince us that God's intentions are not good. Stay the course. Don't give in today. Believe for God's best and don't settle for less.

MEDITATION
Creator of the Stars of Night

Creator of the stars of night,
Thy people's everlasting Light:
O Christ, Redeemer, save us all
And hear Thy servants when they call.

Thou grieving that the Ancient curse
Should doom to death a universe,
Hast found the healing, full of grace,
To cure and save our ruined race.

O Thou, whose coming is with dread
To judge the living and the dead,
Preserve us from the ancient foe
While still we dwell on earth below.

Text: Latin, 5th–10th century

Translated by John Mason Neale, 1818–1866, alt.

Stanzas 1, 2, & 5

P R A Y E R

Father, Creator of the stars of night, I wait for You. You came to me when I was lost and couldn't find my way to You. As I continue this Advent journey, reveal the things I have counted on to fill my heart apart from You and give me the grace to lay them down. I will wait for You and trust You to protect me from my foes and give me all I need. Amen.

JESUS SETS YOU FREE

Isaiah 61:1–3 (NIV)

The Spirit of the Sovereign LORD is on me,
because the LORD has anointed me
to proclaim good news to the poor.
He has sent me to bind up the brokenhearted,
to proclaim freedom for the captives
and release from darkness for the prisoners,
to proclaim the year of the LORD's favor
and the day of vengeance of our God,
to comfort all who mourn,
and provide for those who grieve in Zion—
to bestow on them a crown of beauty
instead of ashes,
the oil of joy
instead of mourning,
and a garment of praise
instead of a spirit of despair.
They will be called oaks of righteousness,
a planting of the LORD
for the display of his splendor.

REFLECTION

In Luke's Gospel Jesus made a powerful declaration when he said the promise spoken in Isaiah 61 was fulfilled through him. He claimed that He was the One who could set the prisoner free. He alone would lift up those who had been trampled by circumstances and shattered dreams. He would cause the blind to see.

So, if you are paralyzed by grief or blinded by anguish, Jesus is the place where healing begins. Even if your life has been reduced to ashes, Jesus has the power to rebuild and restore. Reach out for Him and let Him take your hand. He's not trying to take something from you, but to do something for you. Something He alone can do.

MEDITATION
O Lord, How Shall I Meet You

O Lord, how shall I meet You,
How welcome You aright?
Your people long to greet
You, My hope, my heart's delight!
O kindle, Lord most holy,
Your lamp within my breast
to do in spirit lowly
all that may please You best.

I lay in fetters, groaning;
You came to set me free.
I stood, my shame bemoaning;
You came to honor me.

A glorious crown You give me,
A treasure safe on high
That will not fail or leave me
As earthly riches fly.

Paul Gerhardt, 1607–1676

Stanzas 1 & 3

PRAYER

Father, thank you that your mission all along has been to lift those who have been pounded by the waves of life, to free those imprisoned by addictions, sin and shame. Father, when I felt left behind for dead, discarded and forgotten, You sent Jesus to save my life. Give me the grace to rest in Your freedom today and to trust that you are not finished with me. Amen.

BY HIS WOUNDS
YOU ARE HEALED

Isaiah 53:3–6 (ESV)

He was despised and rejected by men; a man of sorrows, and acquainted with grief; and as one from whom men hide their faces he was despised, and we esteemed him not. Surely he has borne our griefs and carried our sorrows; yet we esteemed him stricken, smitten by God, and afflicted. But he was pierced for our transgressions; he was crushed for our iniquities; upon him was the chastisement that brought us peace, and with his wounds we are healed. We all like sheep have gone astray; we have turned— every one—to his own way; and the LORD has laid on him the iniquity of us all.

REFLECTION

The arrival of Jesus on earth came at a high price. He gave up His rights as God and took on human flesh. And He came with the ulti-mate purpose of being wounded for our sin and shame. Though

Jesus was innocent, He was willing to offer His life as payment for our sin. He was pierced for our wrongs and took our guilt upon Himself.

The price Jesus paid cleared our account of wrong once and for all. Thus, victory over our hurt and pain is not found by delving deeper into our wounds, but by clinging to the wounds of Jesus. He was willing to take the blows and bear the scars. His wounds bring us healing, wholeness, and peace with our God. Every wrong you have done and every wrong that has been done to you has been swallowed up in every right that Jesus has done and in every wrong that has been done to Him. By His wounds you are healed.

MEDITATION
From Depths of Woe I Cry to Thee

From depths of woe I cry to Thee,
In trial and tribulation;
Bend down Thy gracious ear to me,
Lord, hear my supplication.
If Thou rememb'rest ev'ry sin,
Who then could heaven ever win
Or stand before thy presence?

Thy love and grace alone avail
To blot out my transgression;
The best and holiest deeds must fail
To break sin's dread oppression.
Before Thee none can boasting stand,
But all must fear Thy strict demand
And live alone by mercy.

Therefore my hope is in the Lord
And not in mine own merit;
It rests upon His faithful Word
To them of contrite spirit
That He is merciful and just;
This is my comfort and my trust.
His help I wait with patience.

Martin Luther, 1483–1546,

Translated by Catherine Winkworth, 1827–1878, alt.

Stanzas 1–3

PRAYER

Father, thank You for the gift of Your Son, the perfect One given for an imperfect one like me. Thank You that Jesus died the way He died so I can come to You just as I am. Jesus, give me grace to reach for Your scars, believing that when You suffered and bled for me, my wounds were healed. Let Your peace and power cover and heal my heart. Amen.

SEEK AND YOU WILL FIND

Psalm 27:7–14 (NIV)

Hear my voice when I call, LORD;
be merciful to me and answer me.
My heart says of you, "Seek His face!"
Your face, LORD, I will seek.
Do not hide your face from me,
do not turn your servant away in anger;
you have been my helper.
Do not reject me or forsake me,
God my Savior.
Though my father and mother forsake me,
the LORD will receive me.
Teach me your way, LORD;
lead me in a straight path
because of my oppressors.
Do not turn me over to the desire of my foes,
for false witnesses rise up against me,

spouting malicious accusations.
I remain confident of this:
I will see the goodness of the LORD
in the land of the living.
Wait for the LORD;
be strong and take heart
and wait for the LORD.

REFLECTION

God is not hiding from you. Though it may seem like He has dropped off the radar, He is near. Yet to find Him you must patiently seek Him out. Just like you, God wants to be pursued. He wants to know that you believe He is worth searching for. Many say they can't find God; that they can't hear His voice. Yet, are they really seeking Him? If you want to be near God you must create space to seek Him. If you want to know Him, you must start by telling Him. Open His Word and set your gaze on Him. Ask Him to show you who He is. You'll discover that He is waiting to meet you where you are.

Seek and you will find. Knock and the door will be opened to you. Ask and it will be given to you.

MEDITATION
The King Shall Come When Morning Dawns

The King shall come when morning dawns
And light triumphant breaks,
When beauty gilds the eastern hills

And life to joy awakes.

Oh, brighter than the rising morn
When Christ, victorious, rose
And left the lonesome place of death
Despite the rage of foes.

Oh, brighter than that glorious morn
Shall dawn upon our race
The day when Christ in splendor comes
And we shall see His face.

The King shall come when morning dawns
And light and beauty brings.
Hail, Christ the Lord! Your people pray:
Come quickly, King of kings!

John Brownlie, 1857–1925, alt.

Stanzas 1, 3–5

PRAYER

Father, I want to see Your face. Hear my cry and reveal Yourself to me as I make room for You to invade my life. I am desperate for more of You. I am here. I am knocking. Intersect my life today with a greater awareness of who You are. Please show me more of Your character and purpose as I set my heart on You. Amen.

December 2

COMPASSION OVER CONSUMPTION

Today we pause to embrace the true spirit of Christmas.

In the words of the Lord Jesus Himself, "It is more blessed to give than to receive." (Acts 20:35b)

PRAYER

Father, I thank You that You are a giver and not a taker, and You have given so freely to me. Help me see how much I have in You. Please give me the opportunity today to share with someone else what You have so freely entrusted to me. Amen.

IF WE ARE TRULY WAITING ON GOD

WE
WON'T MISS
ANYTHING.

December 3

WHOM SHALL
I FEAR?

Psalm 27:1–6 (NIV)

The LORD is my light and my salvation—
*   whom shall I fear?*
The LORD is the stronghold of my life—
*   of whom shall I be afraid?*
When the wicked advance against me
*   to devour me,*
it is my enemies and my foes
*   who will stumble and fall.*
Though an army besiege me,
*   my heart will not fear;*
though war break out against me,
*   even then I will be confident.*
One thing I ask from the LORD,
*   this only do I seek:*
that I may dwell in the house of the LORD

all the days of my life,
to gaze on the beauty of the LORD
and to seek him in his temple.
For in the day of trouble
he will keep me safe in his dwelling;
he will hide me in the shelter of his sacred tent
and set me high upon a rock.
Then my head will be exalted
above the enemies who surround me;
at his sacred tent I will sacrifice with shouts of joy;
I will sing and make music to the LORD.

REFLECTION

In the midst of the fury and the fray, keep your eyes on Jesus. Emmanuel is near…and He is fighting for you. Though accusations fly and the enemy assaults your thoughts, though people cut you down and drag your name through the mud, though schemes are launched and temptations overwhelm, though your flesh rises up and screams for revenge—your hope is in the One who fights for you. Stand firm in Christ. Show up each day dressed in confidence knowing that the battle belongs to the Lord.

The name of the LORD is a fortified tower; the righteous run to it and are safe (Proverbs 18:10).

MEDITATION
Fear Not to Trust Me in the Storm

Fear not to trust Me in the storm,
I'm always very near.

I come thy needless fears to calm,
Then, weary ones, don't fear.

Refrain
Fear not, I am with thee,
Fear not, I am with thee,
Fear not, I am with thee,
Am with thee all the way.

I may not always seem so near
As thou wouldst have Me be;
But in the calm and in the storm,
I all thy dangers see.

Refrain
Fear not to trust My mighty arm;
It bro't salvation down.
I suffered much to give thee life,
To give to thee a crown.

Refrain

J.W. Howe

Stanzas 1–3

PRAYER

Father, in the middle of the storm I am setting my hope on You. You fight for me and You are greater than all my enemies. Nothing I face today is more powerful than You. You are the solid ground beneath my feet. Thank You for surrounding those who surround me. Give me peace in the presence of my enemies, knowing that You see me and defend me in Your love. Amen.

GOD WILL MAKE A WAY

Isaiah 43:18–19, 20b–21, 25 (NIV)

"Forget the former things; do not dwell on the past. See, I am doing a new thing! Now it springs up; do you not perceive it? I am making a way in the wilderness and streams in the wasteland . . . I provide water in the wilderness and streams in the wasteland, to give drink to my people, my chosen, the people I formed for myself that they may proclaim my praise."

"I, even I, am he who blots out your transgressions, for my own sake, and remembers your sins no more."

REFLECTION

When God led His people out of bondage in Egypt they soon came to what seemed like a dead end at the edge of the Red Sea. The people were so bewildered they cursed God saying, "Could we not have died in Egypt? Did you have to bring us into the wilderness to meet our end?" Yet as it turned out, the desert and the sea were just opportunities for God to show His great power to His people.

It's likely you have felt the same way at times, up against insurmountable odds. But God doesn't even blink at the roadblocks in front of you. In one miraculous motion, He parted the sea before His people and led them through on dry ground. And God can part your "Red Sea" if and when He wants to.

God has already torn down the biggest obstacle we will ever face, the veil of our sin that separated us from His holy embrace. He will, in the same way, lead you through every challenge you will ever face.

MEDITATION
Once He Came in Blessing

Once He came in blessing,
All our sins redressing;
Came in likeness lowly,
Son of God most holy;
Bore the cross to save us;
Hope and freedom gave us.

Come, then, O Lord Jesus,
From our sins release us.
Keep our hearts believing,
That we, grace receiving,
Ever may confess You
Till in heav'n we bless You.

Johann Horn, c. 1490–1547

Translated by Catherine Winkworth, 1827–1878,

Stanzas 1 & 4

Waiting Here for You

PRAYER

Father, I am made by You and formed for Your praise. By Your mercy—and for Your name's sake—You erased my record of sin. I am face-to-face with obstacles where there seems to be no way out, no way forward, and no way through. Yet You have made a way to freedom. I am confident You will lead me through what I am facing today. I will wait in hope for You. Amen.

GLORY IN THE HIGHEST

Psalm 135:13 ESV

Your name, O LORD, endures forever, your renown, O LORD, throughout all ages.

REFLECTION

God has no equal. No rivals. No shortages. No needs. He is before all things and at the end of the day He will be the last one standing. The world is filled with "little g" gods, but our God made the heavens and the earth. No one compares to Him. No one even comes close.

So as you wait on Him today, give Him praise. Maybe your circumstances appear to be upside down, but His throne is decidedly right-side up! Praise Him in the waiting. Exalt Him in the wondering. So don't ask for much today, just keep lifting up the Name above every name. Let that Name ground your heart and still your soul. Let your praise drown out all others who contend for your allegiance and affection. When you do, your very song will lift your thoughts to the very highest place.

MEDITATION
Glory in the Highest

You are the first
You go before
You are the last
Lord, You're the encore
Your name's in lights for all to see
The starry host declare Your glory

Glory in the highest
Glory in the highest
Glory in the highest

Apart from You there is no god
Light of the world
The Bright and Morning Star
Your name will shine for all to see
You are the One
You are my glory

And no one else could ever compare
To You, Lord
All the earth together declares . . .
Glory in the highest . . . to You, Lord

All the earth will sing Your praise
The moon and stars, the sun and rain
Every nation will proclaim
That You are God and You will reign

Glory, glory hallelujah
Glory, glory to You, Lord

Louie Giglio

Glory, glory hallelujah
Hallelujah

Chris Tomlin, Matt Redman, Jesse Reeves,
Daniel Carson, Ed Cash

PRAYER

Father, what shall I say to You? You have no equal or rival. My words and my thoughts are so small when compared to You. I have seen the starry night and it cannot hold a candle to Your glory. Expand my faith and give me words as I seek to join the anthem of Your praise.

All praise is Yours, now and forever. I will walk in that truth today. I will believe it. And act like it. And pray like it. And give like it. And praise like there is none like You. Amen!

Waiting Here for You

HOPE WHEN WE CAN'T HOLD ON

Isaiah 40:27–31 (NIV)

Why do you complain, Jacob?
Why do you say, Israel,
"My way is hidden from the LORD;
my cause is disregarded by my God"?
Do you not know?
Have you not heard?
The LORD is the everlasting God,
the Creator of the ends of the earth.
He will not grow tired or weary,
and his understanding no one can fathom.
He gives strength to the weary
and increases the power of the weak.
Even youths grow tired and weary,
and young men stumble and fall;
but those who hope in the LORD
will renew their strength.

They will soar on wings like eagles;
they will run and not grow weary,
they will walk and not be faint.

REFLECTION

There are times in the waiting where you can start to think you've dropped off God's radar. In the chaos and confusion you begin to think you've fallen through the cracks, or worse, been completely forgotten by God. From your vantage point there's only silence.

But God has not forgotten you…or His promise. God is there, even in the darkness. If you feel like you can't make it one more step, or if you've already stumbled and hit the deck, He is holding out His hand. Just reach for Him and know He's holding on to you. Even when you are falling, hope in the Lord, stand on His promise. No matter what the circumstance, you will find new strength—His strength—to breathe one more breath.

MEDITATION
Let the Earth Now Praise the Lord

Let the earth now praise the Lord,
Who has truly kept His word
And at last to us did send
Christ, the sinner's help and friend.
Bruise for me the serpent's head
That, set free from doubt and dread,
I may cling to You in faith,

Safely kept through life and death.

Then when You will come again
As the glorious king to reign,
I with joy will see Your face,
Freely ransomed by Your grace.

Heinrich Held, 1620–1659;

Translated by Catherine Winkworth, 1827–1878, alt.

PRAYER

Father, bring me through the fire and rising tide. You have given the Holy Christ in exchange for my life. Will You not also, with Him, freely give me all things? I am clinging to You and waiting in expectation. Don't let me sink. Hold on to me. Amen.

December 7

BE STILL

A time of stillness as we wait in hope on the Lord.

Psalm 46:10–11 (ESV)

"Be still, and know that I am God. I will be exalted among the nations, I will be exalted in the earth!" The LORD of hosts is with us; the God of Jacob is our fortress.

REFLECTION

Quiet moments are rare and it can be difficult to find stillness, but take a few minutes today to quietly and deeply consider the Lord. Try not to read or study or be distracted—just be still and meditate on the person of Jesus and all He has done for you. Think about His birth, His infancy, and the dawn of light rising over a dark and weary world. Think about His death and sacrifice, and the gift of life He extends to you. Meditate on His resurrection, His power over the darkness and the grave. Drink in His presence and in the stillness seek His face. And think about His coming, the day you will see Him face to face.

Louie Giglio

MEDITATION

Take a moment and just be quiet before Him. Think about Jesus and take confidence in Him.

PRAYER

Father, I am waiting here for You. Meet me in the silence. Meet me in this moment. Meet me in and through Your Son and by Your Spirit. Amen.

IN THE VALLEY OF DEATH, YOU ARE THERE

Psalm 23:4a (ESV)

Even though I walk through the valley of the shadow of death, I will fear no evil, *for you are with me.*

1 Corinthians 15:55–56 (NIV)

"Where, O death, is your victory?
Where, O death, is your sting?"
The sting of death is sin, and the power of sin is the law. But thanks be to God! He gives us the victory through our Lord Jesus Christ.

REFLECTION

There is no place of waiting and wondering like the graveside. The final crushing blow of death is real. Yet, even at the grave, God is near. In fact, especially at the grave, God is close to us. And God understands.

Not only has God suffered the death of His own Son, while on earth Jesus experienced the physical death of those He loved. He knows what you are going through and the loss you feel. He is very much in touch with your grief. He understands the agony of death.

Jesus faced death and the grave. He suffered and died. Yet, through Jesus the grave is overwhelmed. For those who hope in Him, death does not have the final say. Though the valley of mourning and loss are daunting and frightening, Jesus is in the valley with you. Walk with Him. He will lead you through and His presence will be enough for you.

MEDITATION
Low In the Grave He Lay

Low in the grave He lay, Jesus my Savior!
Waiting the coming day, Jesus my Lord!

Refrain
Up from the grave He arose,
With a mighty triumph o'er His foes,
He arose a Victor from the dark domain,
And He lives forever, with His saints to reign.
He arose! He arose!
Hallelujah! Christ arose!

Vainly they watch His bed, Jesus my Savior!
Vainly they seal the dead, Jesus my Lord!

Refrain
Death cannot keep its Prey, Jesus my Savior!
He tore the bars away, Jesus my Lord!

Refrain

Robert Lowry, 1826–1899

PRAYER

Father, give me grace as I mourn the loss of those I love. Thank You for being more powerful than death. Because I trust in You, I know the grave will not be my final resting place. When You rose from the dead, I was also freed from death's grip. Because You are alive, I am alive in You. Amen.

COMPASSION OVER CONSUMPTION

Today we pause to embrace the true spirit of Christmas.

In the words of the Lord Jesus Himself, "It is more blessed to give than to receive." (Acts 20:35b)

PRAYER

Father, I thank You that You are a giver and not a taker, and You have given so freely to me. Help me see how much I have in You. Please give me the opportunity today to share with someone else what You so freely entrusted to me. Amen.

WHILE WE ARE WAITING *ON GOD* WE ARE WAITING *WITH GOD.*

GOD

IS

THERE

THE

WHOLE

TIME.

GOD GIVES ALL GOOD THINGS

Psalm 127:1–2 (NIV)

Unless the LORD builds the house, the builders labor in vain. Unless the LORD watches over the city, the guards stand watch in vain. In vain you rise early and stay up late, toiling for food to eat— for he grants sleep to those he loves.

James 1:17 (NIV)

Every good and perfect gift is from above, coming down from the Father of the heavenly lights, who does not change like shifting shadows.

REFLECTION

Often we feel like everybody else is getting ahead, getting what they want; or worse, getting what we want! But God's gifts for you will come at just the right time.

God is the giver of life and breath. And with these God gives to every creature what they need. A tiny sparrow does not fall from the sky without Him noticing. And He clothes the hillside with an array of beauty and vibrant color. You are His beloved—His son or daughter by faith in Christ. Trust your perfect Father's heart. He will give you exactly what you need, and as you seek Him, He will even give you the desires of your heart.

If you're truly waiting on God, you won't miss anything. When you walk with God, you always arrive on time.

MEDITATION
Of the Father's Love Begotten

Of the Father's love begotten,
Ere the worlds began to be,
He is Alpha and Omega;
He the source, the ending He,
Of the things that are,
that have been,
And that future years shall see,
Evermore and evermore.

Oh, that birth forever blessed
When the virgin, full of grace,
By the Holy Ghost conceiving,
Bore the Savior of our race,
And the babe,
the world's Redeemer,
First revealed His sacred face,
Evermore and evermore.

Louie Giglio

This is He whom seers in old time
Chanted of with one accord,
Whom the voices of the prophets
Promised in their faithful word.
New He shines,
The long-expected.
Let creation praise its Lord,
Evermore and evermore.

Aurelius Prudentius Clemens, 348–410

Translated by John Mason Neale, 1818–1866

PRAYER

Father, give me rest today knowing that when I walk with You, I will never miss out on anything. Give me the grace to do my best, but give me the peace that comes from knowing every good thing comes from You. Amen.

WHERE OUR SONG COMES FROM

Psalm 40:1–5 (NIV)

I waited patiently for the LORD; he turned to me and heard my cry. He lifted me out of the slimy pit, out of the mud and mire; he set my feet on a rock and gave me a firm place to stand. He put a new song in my mouth, a hymn of praise to our God. Many will see and fear the Lord and put their trust in him. Blessed is the one who trusts in the Lord, who does not look to the proud, to those who turn aside to false gods. Many, Lord my God, are the wonders you have done, the things you planned for us. None can compare with you; were I to speak and tell of your deeds, they would be too many to declare.

REFLECTION

The Gospel is the stunning story of Christ coming into the world to lift us from the mess, to set us on solid ground with Him. And when He raised us up, He gave us something to sing about. He replaced the old songs of despair with new songs of praise—songs for the One who makes us new.

The Gospel and worship are inseparably linked. We don't worship Jesus because we *ought to;* we give Him praise because of who He is…and because He has brought us back to life! And best of all—we don't have to wait for the band to start playing. We have God's mercy, and that's all the music we will ever need! So if you're alive today, sing redemption's song. If you have been set free, sing the name of the One who freed you.

God's grace is the soil from which worship springs. Savor His grace. Grow your praise. Turn your waiting into worshiping. God is worthy of it, and you'll be amazed at how your outlook shifts to the rhythm of His song.

MEDITATION
Oh, Holy Night

Oh, holy night, the stars are brightly shining;
It is the night of the dear Savior's birth!
Long lay the world in sin and error pining,
Till He appeared and the soul felt its worth.
A thrill of hope, the weary soul rejoices,
For yonder breaks a new and glorious morn.

Fall on your knees, oh, hear the angel voices!
Oh, night divine, oh, night when Christ was born!
Oh, night divine, oh, night, oh, night divine!
O night, O holy night, O night divine!

Waiting Here for You

Truly He taught us to love one another;
His law is love and His Gospel is peace.
Chains shall He break for the slave is our brother,
And in His Name all oppression shall cease.
Sweet hymns of joy in grateful chorus raise we,
Let all within us praise His holy Name!

Christ is the Lord!
Oh, praise His name forever!
His pow'r and glory evermore proclaim!
His pow'r and glory evermore proclaim!

Placide Cappeau, 1808–1877

Music by Adolphe Charles Adams, 1803–1856

PRAYER

Father, thank You for hearing my cry from the pit. I receive Your grace today and stand on the solid ground of Your righteousness. Every time I think of how You rescued me, my mouth can't help but sing Your praise. I love You and am so grateful for You. Let my whole life sing Your song. Amen!

GOODBYE CONDEMNATION

Romans 8:1–4 (NIV)

Therefore, there is now no condemnation for those who are in Christ Jesus, because through Christ Jesus the law of the Spirit who gives life has set you free from the law of sin and death. For what the law was powerless to do because it was weakened by the flesh, God did by sending his own Son in the likeness of sinful flesh to be a sin offering. And so he condemned sin in the flesh, in order that the righteous requirement of the law might be fully met in us, who do not live according to the flesh but according to the Spirit.

REFLECTION

To embrace the birth, life, death, and resurrection of Christ is to agree with God. Your debt is paid; your guilt is gone. What's done is done. Jesus bore the guilt and shame on His innocent life and paid the price in full. It is finished. When the voice of the accuser comes, remind him of what the Redeemer has done, and say, "Goodbye, condemnation.

I am free!"

Scripture says God has removed your sins as far as the east is from the west. Think about how far that is. There is no limit to His forgiveness. He remembers your sin no more. That doesn't mean God doesn't know you sinned. It means that, even though He does know about all your wrong, He is not holding your sins against you and will never use them to accuse you again. Because Christ was condemned for our sins, condemnation has got to go. That is why the gift of God is called amazing grace.

MEDITATION
The Day is Surely Drawing Near

My Savior paid the debt I owe
And for my sin was smitten;
Within the Book of Life I know
My name has now been written.
I will not doubt, for I am free
And Satan cannot threaten me;
There is no condemnation!
May Christ our intercessor be
And through His blood and merit
Read from His book that we are free
With all who life inherit.
Then we shall see Him face to face,
With all His saints in that blest place
Which He has purchased for us.

Bartholomäus Ringwaldt, 1532–1599

Translated by Philip A. Peter, 1832–1919, alt.

Louie Giglio

PRAYER

Father, You paid it all, and I believe it. I will walk in the freedom You won for me. I declare it in the face of my enemy: I AM FREE. Let my life be my thanks and praise to You. Amen.

DON'T COUNT GOD OUT

2 Peter 3:8–16a (ESV)

But do not overlook this one fact, beloved, that with the Lord one day is as a thousand years, and a thousand years as one day. The Lord is not slow to fulfill his promise as some count slowness, but is patient toward you, not wishing that any should perish, but that all should reach repentance. But the day of the Lord will come like a thief, and then the heavens will pass away with a roar, and the heavenly bodies will be burned up and dissolved, and the earth and the works that are done on it will be exposed.

Since all these things are thus to be dissolved, what sort of people ought you to be in lives of holiness and godliness, waiting for and hastening the coming of the day of God, because of which the heavens will be set on fire and dissolved, and the heavenly bodies will melt as they burn! But according to his promise we are waiting for new heavens and a new earth in which righteousness dwells.

Therefore, beloved, since you are waiting for these, be diligent to be found by him without spot or blemish, and at peace. And count the patience of our Lord as salvation, just as our beloved brother Paul also wrote to you according to the wisdom given him, as he does in all his letters when he speaks in them of these matters.

REFLECTION

God is not slow. He is merciful. Every day in which He waits to blast the final trumpet and bring an end to life as we know it is a day of extended grace that more people may trust in Him. It is a day for more people to hear of His love, trust in His promise, forsake evil ways, and put their hope in Jesus.

The day is coming when sin will be done away with and the earth will be restored to its perfect fullness. But God is patient, waiting for all those He loves to find their way to Him. Again today His arms are open wide for all who will come home to His embrace. But, make no mistake. God is coming. The enemy will be cast out. All things will be made new. Live ready, but embrace the pain, knowing your hardship extends God's grace for one more day.

MEDITATION
O Come, O Come, Emmanuel

O come, O come, Emmanuel,
And ransom captive Israel,
That mourns in lonely exile here
Until the Son of God appear.

Rejoice! Rejoice!
Emmanuel shall come to thee, O Israel.

O come, Thou Wisdom from on high,
Who orderest all things mightily;
To us the path of knowledge show,
And teach us in her ways to go.

Rejoice! Rejoice!
Emmanuel shall come to thee, O Israel.

Latin, c. 12th century

Psalteriolum Cantionum Catholicarum, Köln, 1710

Translated by John Mason Neale, 1818–1866, alt.

Stanzas 1 & 2

PRAYER

Father, shake me from my slumber. Forgive me when I accuse You of failing to keep Your promises. Thank You for today, a fresh gift of grace. May I use it well to speak of Your mercy and extend Your Gospel, as I wait for You. Amen.

JESUS IS OUR FEAST

John 6:35–40 (NIV)

Then Jesus declared, "I am the bread of life. Whoever comes to me will never go hungry, and whoever believes in me will never be thirsty. But as I told you, you have seen me and still you do not believe. All those the Father gives me will come to me, and whoever comes to me I will never drive away. For I have come down from heaven not to do my will but to do the will of him who sent me. And this is the will of him who sent me, that I shall lose none of all those he has given me, but raise them up at the last day. For my Father's will is that everyone who looks to the Son and believes in him shall have eternal life, and I will raise them up at the last day."

REFLECTION

Jesus doesn't just give you what you need; Jesus *is* what you need. Your heart was created by Him, for Him. You can fight and claw to gain the world, but without Jesus, you will never be completely satisfied.

If there is a growing discontent deep inside your heart—a hunger that hasn't been completely satisfied by the people, pleasures, parties, material things, or accomplishments—today is the day to open your heart to the idea that it is Jesus that you were made for. But you have to walk away from "less," and ask Him to become your "more." Jesus is enough for you, and He is here.

MEDITATION
O Come, O Come, Emmanuel

O come, O come, Emmanuel,
And ransom captive Israel
That mourns in lonely exile here
Until the Son of God appear.

Rejoice! Rejoice!
Emmanuel shall come to thee, O Israel.

O come, O Branch of Jesse's stem,
Unto your own and rescue them!
From depths of hell your people save,
And give them victory o'er the grave.

Rejoice! Rejoice!
Emmanuel shall come to thee, O Israel.

Latin, c. 12th century

Psalteriolum Cantionum Catholicarum, Köln, 1710

Translated by John Mason Neale, 1818–1866, alt.

Stanzas 1 & 4

PRAYER

Father, You alone know how hard I have searched for satisfaction in the people and things of this world. But they are broken, and I am too. You alone can fill my hungry heart. You alone have the love that is like no other. You never change. Open my eyes today. Show me Your riches and glory. Help me know You more. Let me see the feast of that is set before me, so I may delight myself in You alone. Amen.

NOT YET HOME

John 14:1–7 (NIV)

"Do not let your hearts be troubled. You believe in God; believe also in me. My Father's house has many rooms; if that were not so, would I have told you that I am going there to prepare a place for you? And if I go and prepare a place for you, I will come back and take you to be with me that you also may be where I am. You know the way to the place where I am going." Thomas said to him, "Lord, we don't know where you are going, so how can we know the way?" Jesus answered, "I am the way and the truth and the life. No one comes to the Father except through me. If you really know me, you will know my Father as well. From now on, you do know him and have seen him."

REFLECTION

Don't settle down today as if earth is your retirement home. You, my friend, are just passing through. Everything you see is passing away. Perhaps the greatest tragedy of all is to live as if this world is all there is, when God's promise is for so much more.

So make the most of every moment while you're here. If you see something wrong, seek to fix it, but as you do, know that Jesus is preparing something brand new (and exponentially better) for those who have put their hope in Him. Live like you are headed to forever. Endure like you believe this world will fade, but Jesus will remain.

MEDITATION
O Come, O Come, Emmanuel

O come, O come, Emmanuel,
And ransom captive Israel
That mourns in lonely exile here
Until the Son of God appear.

Rejoice! Rejoice!
Emmanuel shall come to thee, O Israel.

O come, O Key of David, come
And open wide our heavenly home.
Make safe for us the heavenward road
And bar the way to death's abode.

Rejoice! Rejoice!
Emmanuel shall come to you, O Israel.

Latin, c. 12th century

Psalteriolum Cantionum Catholicarum, Köln, 1710

Translated by John Mason Neale, 1818–1866, alt.

Stanzas 1 & 5

PRAYER

Father, I need Your help today. It's tempting to believe that what I *see* is all there is. Yet, I know this present earth is not my true home. Give me the grace to travel light and the wisdom to invest in the things that last forever. Free me from living as if *this is it,* and lead me to that precious city where You reign. Amen.

Louie Giglio

COMPASSION OVER CONSUMPTION

Today we pause to embrace the true spirit of Christmas.

In the words of the Lord Jesus Himself, "It is more blessed to give than to receive." (Acts 20:35b)

PRAYER

Father, I thank You that You are a giver and not a taker, and You have given so freely to me. Help me see how much I have in You. Please give me the opportunity today to share with someone else what You so freely entrusted to me. Amen.

WHO YOU BECOME WHILE YOU ARE WAITING IS AS IMPORTANT AS WHAT YOU ARE WAITING FOR.

—*Nicky Gumble*

NO OTHER NAME

Philippians 2:5–11 (NIV)

In your relationships with one another, have the same mindset as Christ Jesus: Who, being in very nature God, did not consider equality with God something to be used to his own advantage; rather, he made himself nothing by taking the very nature of a servant, being made in human likeness. And being found in appearance as a man, he humbled himself by becoming obedient to death–even death on a cross! Therefore God exalted him to the highest place and gave him the name that is above every name, that at the name of Jesus every knee should bow, in heaven and on earth and under the earth, and every tongue acknowledge that Jesus Christ is Lord, to the glory of God the Father.

REFLECTION

Christmas led to the Cross, and on both days Jesus accomplished what no one else could. There is no one like Him—no one even comes close. No name on this earth can be mentioned in the same sentence with His. He is Supreme. Stellar. Significant. Sturdy. He stands the test of time…and then some.

Jesus has the Name that makes demons tremble. The Name that vanquishes death. The Name that breaks iron bars. The Name that sets prisoners free. Jesus is the highest and the most honorable of all. Jesus alone is holy. He trumps everything and everyone. And anyone who thinks differently is a fool for doing so. The Name of Jesus awakens the dead, and gives them life. His Name awakens the dawn and ushers in the night.

And this Name He has given to all who believe in Him. For all who call on the name of Jesus, will be saved.

MEDITATION
O Come, All Ye Faithful

O come, all ye faithful,
Joyful and triumphant;
O come ye; O come ye to Bethlehem!
Come, and behold Him,
Born the King of Angels!
O come, let us adore Him;
O come, let us adore Him;
O come, let us adore Him;
Christ, the Lord!

Sing, choirs of angels;
Sing in exultation;
Sing, all ye citizens of heaven above!

Glory to God, all glory in the highest!
O come, let us adore Him;
O come, let us adore Him;
O come, let us adore Him;
Christ, the Lord!

Yea, Lord, we greet thee,
Born this happy morning;
Jesus, to thee be all glory given;
Word of the Father, now in flesh appearing!
O come, let us adore Him;
O come, let us adore Him;
O come, let us adore Him;
Christ, the Lord!

Written by John Francis Wade, 1711–1786

Translated by Frederick Oakeley

Stanzas 1, 3, 4

PRAYER

Father, thank You for the Name of Jesus. Jesus, there is no other name like Yours. You humbly came and laid Your life down. Now You are exalted to the highest place of all. I bend my knees to You today. Your Name alone sets me free. I want my life and breath to make much of the Name that is greater than all others. Amen.

December 18

HUMILITY LOOKS GOOD ON EVERYONE

James 4:6 (NIV)

But he gives us more grace. That is why Scripture says: "God opposes the proud but shows favor to the humble."

1 Peter 5:5b–7 (ESV)

Clothe yourselves, all of you, with humility toward one another, for "God opposes the proud but gives grace to the humble." Humble yourselves, therefore, under the mighty hand of God so that at the proper time he may exalt you, casting all your anxieties on him, because he cares for you.

REFLECTION

Jesus is the King of Kings, yet He arrived as a humble servant. Though escorted by angels, He arrived on earth wrapped in humility. So many

Louie Giglio

times we miss the mark when we think of what humility is really about. Humility is not thinking you are less, it is never forgetting the fact that it is Jesus who made you more. So, how do you become like Jesus? How do you develop a spirit of humility?

Humility is the byproduct of being with Jesus. Anyone who walks intimately with Him will not think more highly of himself than he should. To be loved by Jesus and invited into a relationship with Him, is all we need to right-size ourselves and to take on *His* gentleness and grace.

To be humble doesn't mean you have to be weak. God has given you all you need to live confidently as His child. The proud refuse to lift up God's name in praise. Yet He raises the humble to new heights.

MEDITATION AND PRAYER
A Private Litany of Humility

From the desire of being praised, deliver me, Jesus.
From the desire of being honored, deliver me, Jesus.

From the desire of being preferred, deliver me, Jesus.
From the desire of being consulted, deliver me, Jesus.
From the desire of being approved, deliver me, Jesus.

From the desire of comfort and ease, deliver me, Jesus.
From the fear of being humiliated, deliver me, Jesus.
From the fear of being criticized, deliver me, Jesus.
From the fear of being passed over, deliver me, Jesus.
From the fear of being forgotten, deliver me, Jesus.
From the fear of being lonely, deliver me, Jesus.

Louie Giglio

From the fear of being hurt, deliver me, Jesus.
From the fear of suffering, deliver me, Jesus.

That others may be loved more than I,
Jesus, grant me the grace to desire it.
That others may be chosen and I set aside,
Jesus, grant me the grace to desire it.
That others may be praised and I unnoticed,
Jesus, grant me the grace to desire it.

O Jesus, meek and humble of heart, make my heart like yours.
O Jesus, meek and humble of heart, strengthen me with your Spirit.
O Jesus, meek and humble of heart, teach me your ways.

O Jesus, meek and humble of heart,
help me put my self-importance aside
to learn the kind of cooperation with others
that makes possible the presence of your Abba's household. Amen.

Adapted from a prayer by Rafael,

Cardinal Merry Del Val, 1865–1930

December 19

COMPASSION OVER CONSUMPTION

Today we pause to embrace the true spirit of Christmas.

In the words of the Lord Jesus Himself, "It is more blessed to give than to receive." (Acts 20:35b)

PRAYER

Father, I thank You that You are a giver and not a taker, and You have given so freely to me. Help me see how much I have in You. Please give me the opportunity today to share with someone else what You so freely entrusted to me. Amen.

LIGHT OF THE WORLD

Isaiah 9:2–3, 6 (NIV)

The people walking in darkness have seen a great light; on those living in the land of deep darkness a light has dawned. You have enlarged the nation and increased their joy; they rejoice before you as people rejoice at the harvest, as warriors rejoice when dividing the plunder . . . For to us a child is born, to us a son is given, and the government will be on his shoulders. And he will be called Wonderful Counselor, Mighty God, Everlasting Father, Prince of Peace.

REFLECTION

There is no doubt we are living in dark times. Violence and injustice are everywhere. People hurt themselves and hurt those around them. Nations war, captives are taken, the innocent suffer, and the earth itself rages with tempests, earthquakes, floods, and famine.

This is the residue of sin on planet earth. Things are broken. People are hurting. The night is here. Darkness is upon us. Yet shining in the night is a Savior, and He has come to shine on you. In fact, Scripture says that He gives His light to all who trust in Him.

Christ has come, and He has come to *you*. Thus, He's setting you – and His church – on a hill for all to see. Look for the darkness and head that way. Seek out injustice and right it. Speak into violence and make peace. That is how He will shine brightest, and is needed most.

MEDITATION
O Come, O Come, Emmanuel

O come, O come, Emmanuel,
And ransom captive Israel
That mourns in lonely exile here
Until the Son of God appear.

Rejoice! Rejoice!
Emmanuel shall come to thee, O Israel!

O come, O Dayspring from on high,
And cheer us by your drawing nigh;
Disperse the gloomy clouds of night,
And death's dark shadow put to flight.

Rejoice! Rejoice!
Emmanuel shall come to thee, O Israel!

Latin, c. 12th century
Psalteriolum Cantionum Catholicarum, Köln, 1710
Translated by John Mason Neale, 1818–1866, alt.
Stanzas 1 & 6

Louie Giglio

PRAYER

Father, You are everlasting; You are a light for the nations. Arise and shine in and through me, for the night grows long. Give me patience and strength to be faithful until the light of Your kingdom fills the sky. By Your grace and according to Your mercy, open the eyes of those who walk in darkness. Help me not be one who constantly runs into the safety of the light. Give me boldness to proclaim the light I have found in You in the darkest places. Amen.

PREPARING THE WAY

Luke 1:67–79 (NIV)

The prayer of Zechariah at the birth of his son, John, who would be a messenger sent from God to prepare the way for Jesus:

His father Zechariah was filled with the Holy Spirit and prophesied: "Praise be to the Lord, the God of Israel, because he has come to his people and redeemed them. He has raised up a horn of salvation for us in the house of his servant David (as he said through his holy prophets of long ago), salvation from our enemies and from the hand of all who hate us—to show mercy to our ancestors and to remember his holy covenant, the oath he swore to our father Abraham: to rescue us from the hand of our enemies, and to enable us to serve him without fear in holiness and righteousness before him all our days. And you, my child, will be called a prophet of the Most High; for you will go on before the Lord to prepare the way for him, to give His people the knowledge of salvation through the forgiveness of their sins, because of the tender mercy of our God, by which the rising sun will come to us from heaven to shine on those living in darkness and in the shadow of death, to guide our feet into the path of peace."

REFLECTION

When God gets ready to do something great, He prepares the way. One thing leads to another and when the time is right, God arrives to do what only He can do. So don't be bogged down today by the hard work of building roads for those around you. Remove the stones where you can. Pave a smooth path when you have the opportunity.

You may not get to see the harvest every time, but you can plant the seed. You may not be there when your friend puts her faith in Jesus, but you can play your part by telling her about His love. With God, nothing is wasted. Some plant, others water, and still others harvest. Sometimes we get to do all three. But every time, it is God who is doing the work to bring the increase.

What can you do today to show someone the way toward freedom and life? Think of yourself as a way-maker God is using to make paths that will help others see and savor Jesus more.

MEDITATION
O Come, O Come, Emmanuel

O come, O come, Emmanuel,
And ransom captive Israel
That mourns in lonely exile here
Until the Son of God appear.

Rejoice! Rejoice!
Emmanuel shall come to thee, O Israel!

O come, Desire of nations, bind
In one the hearts of humankind;
O bid thou our sad divisions cease,
And be for us our King of Peace.

Rejoice! Rejoice!
Emmanuel shall come to thee, O Israel!

Latin, c. 12th century

Psalteriolum Cantionum Catholicarum, Köln, 1710

Translated by John Mason Neale, 1818–1866, alt.

Stanzas 1 & 7

PRAYER

Father, I praise You for coming and leading me out of dark places, into the light of Your love. I renounce everything that opposes You and seeks to separate us. Unite mankind in Your peace. Give me love for all people. Come, Emmanuel, and be with me. Christ in me, my peace. Amen.

MAN'S DECREE.
GOD'S DESIGN.

Luke 2:1–14 (NIV)

In those days Caesar Augustus issued a decree that a census should be taken of the entire Roman world. (This was the first census that took place while Quirinius was governor of Syria.) And everyone went to their own town to register. So Joseph also went up from the town of Nazareth in Galilee to Judea, to Bethlehem the town of David, because he belonged to the house and line of David. He went there to register with Mary, who was pledged to be married to him and was expecting a child. While they were there, the time came for the baby to be born, and she gave birth to her firstborn, a son. She wrapped him in cloths and placed him in a manger, because there was no guest room available for them. And there were shepherds living out in the fields nearby, keeping watch over their flocks at night. An angel of the Lord appeared to them, and the glory of the Lord shone around them, and they were terrified. But the angel said to them, "Do not be afraid. I bring you good news that will cause great joy for all the people. Today in the town of David a Savior has been born to you; he is the Messiah, the Lord. This will be a sign to you: You will find a baby wrapped in cloths and lying in a manger."

Suddenly a great company of the heavenly host appeared with the angel, praising God and saying,

> *"Glory to God in the highest heaven,*
> *and on earth peace to those on whom his favor rests."*

REFLECTION

Caesar was the most powerful man in the world at the time of Christ's birth. A single edict from his hand propelled Mary and Joseph on a journey to Bethlehem to pay their taxes. And yet, looking back, it is clear that Caesar wasn't the mastermind calling the shots. God was using Caesar to make way for Christmas! God was using Caesar's decree to align heavenly plans. Thank God for Caesar's decree!

As today unfolds around you, remember that man may make laws, but God designs days. No person or power can trump God's plans for your life. He is ordering all things to fulfill His purpose and His promise for you.

MEDITATION
Whate'er my God Ordains is Right

What God ordains is always good:
His will is just and holy.
As He directs my life for me,
I follow meek and lowly.
My God indeed
In ev'ry need
Knows well how He will shield me;
To Him, then, I will yield me.

What God ordains is always good:
He never will deceive me;
He leads me in His righteous way,
And never will He leave me.
I take content

What He has sent;
His hand that sends me sadness
Will turn my tears to gladness.

What God ordains is always good:
His loving thought attends me;
No poison can be in the cup
That my physician sends me.
My God is true;
Each morning new
I trust His grace unending,
My life to Him commending.

Samuel Rodigast, 1649–1708

Stanzas 1–3

PRAYER

Father, I'll praise Your Name forever. All other names will flicker and fade, and rulers great and small will be forgotten, but Your Name I will praise for eternity. Help me see today that men may have power, but You call all the shots. I trust You today. You alone are God. You alone are worthy. Amen.

HOPE RISING

John 3:16–18 (NIV)

For God so loved the world that he gave his one and only Son, that whoever believes in him shall not perish but have eternal life. For God did not send his Son into the world to condemn the world, but to save the world through him. Whoever believes in him is not condemned, but whoever does not believe stands condemned already because they have not believed in the name of God's one and only Son.

REFLECTION

Take a moment of silence to reflect on everything you have experienced on your Advent journey. Tomorrow the Church celebrates the dawn of grace in the coming of Jesus—the only Person who chose to be born. He arrived amidst the sheep of Bethlehem as they were being raised to serve as sacrifices at Jerusalem's temple.

Thirty-three years later, and just six miles from where He was born, Jesus would be the last of Bethlehem's sheep. Crucified for your sins, dead and buried, Christ would come back to life three days later.

Though we are still longing to experience everything God has promised and we wait for our ultimate redemption—one wait is already over. Christ has come. Our sins are forgiven. Death has been defeated. Love has won!

MEDITATION
What Child is This

What Child is this, who, laid to rest,
On Mary's lap is sleeping?
Whom angels greet with anthems sweet,
While shepherds watch are keeping?
This, this is Christ, the King,
Whom shepherds guard and angels sing:
Haste, haste to bring Him laud,
The Babe, the Son of Mary!

Why lies He in such mean estate,
Where ox and ass are feeding?
Good Christian, fear: for sinners here
The silent Word is pleading.
Nails, spear, shall pierce Him through;
The cross be borne for me, for you.
Hail, hail, the Word made flesh,
The Babe, the Son of Mary!

So bring Him incense, gold and myrrh,
Come, peasant, king to own Him.
The King of kings salvation brings;

Louie Giglio

Let loving hearts enthrone Him.
Raise, raise the song on high,
The virgin sings her lullaby.
Joy, joy, for Christ is born,
The Babe, the Son of Mary!

William Chatterton Dix, 1837–1898

Stanzas 1–3

PRAYER

Father, You have brought me this far in hopeful expectation. I am confident Your mighty hand and great power are sufficient to lead me all the way home. Awaken my heart more and more to You. Live in me. Christ with me. For Your glory. Amen.

A SAVIOR IS BORN

Psalm 8:9 (ESV)

O LORD, our Lord, how majestic is your name in all the earth!

REFLECTION

On this night, shepherds were doing what they always did, keeping an eye on Bethlehem's sheep through the night. But everything was about to change, as heaven opened and the angel of the Lord appeared to them and declared that Jesus had been born nearby.

What irony. The sheep these shepherds were raising would be sacrificed just a few miles down the road on Jerusalem's altar. Yet the shepherds themselves could not enter the temple to worship even if they wanted to. Because of their profession, they were ceremonially unclean. They were outcasts in the very worship that their hands made possible.

Yet, God chose the shepherds to receive the greatest news ever heard. God came to them because He knew the shepherds couldn't make it to *church.* What does that say about the Gospel? What does it say about you?

This magnificent night says that grace meets you where you are, and saves you while you cannot do a thing to save yourself. Tonight, celebrate that Christ has come. Not to a mansion, but a manger. Not to the high and mighty, but to the guys on the lowest rung of the spiritual ladder. And celebrate that God's grace finds you wherever you are this Christmas and shows you the way upwards to the arms of Almighty God.

MEDITATION FOR CHRISTMAS EVE
Silent Night, Holy Night

Silent night, holy night!
All is calm, all is bright
'Round yon virgin, mother and child.
Holy Infant, so tender and mild,
Sleep in heavenly peace,
Sleep in heavenly peace.

Silent night, holy night!
Shepherds quake at the sight;
Glories stream from heaven afar,
Heavenly hosts sing "Alleluia:
Christ the Savior is born;
Christ the Savior is born!"

Silent night, holy night!
Son of God, love's pure light
Radiant beams from thy holy face,
With the dawn of redeeming grace,

Jesus, Lord, at thy birth,
Jesus, Lord, at thy birth.

Words: Joseph Mohr, 1792–1848.

Music: Franz Gruber, 1787–1863

Stanzas 1–3

PRAYER

Father, it's just You and me in this silent moment. In the stillness, I know You are near—and You are all I need. Thank You for stepping down from heaven to earth through Your Son, Jesus Christ. I'm so grateful for Your mission of love to people who could never earn or deserve it—people like me. I receive Your amazing, unconditional love. Though a babe, Jesus, You were Lord at Your birth. Angels escorted You as You arrived in the manger. Kings bowed down before You. I, too, surrender my life to You. I give You the good and the bad . . . everything. I'm trusting You with my present and my future. Servant-King Jesus, be Lord in my heart today. Amen.

Aaron's mom lay beneath the blankets, her body frail. Aaron slipped around the end of the bed where he could see her face. Her eyes were closed and she was motionless, except for her steady, labored breathing.

"She is having a lot of trouble breathing on her own." Dr. Amer stood in the doorway. "It began last night and, at this point, I'm afraid there is nothing I can do."

Aaron nodded. "I thought she was going to be awake."

"I'm sorry. Her eyes were open a few minutes ago, but her body is exhausted. We are making her as comfortable as possible."

Dr. Amer paused, and Aaron knew what was coming.

"I think it would be good for you to call your family and let them know."

She had been fighting so hard for so long, the inevitable actually felt like it would never happen. Was *this* finally going to be the day?

"I'll leave you alone," Dr. Amer said.

Aaron nodded again, but didn't take his eyes off his mom's face.

He stayed by her side for a few minutes, holding her hand and stroking her forehead, and then walked back to the hallway to call his brother and sister.

He dialed Anna but she didn't pick up. He didn't want to leave a message and called his brother instead.

Matt said he would get to the airport as fast as he could, but flying standby was the best he could manage on Christmas Eve. On top of that, a massive winter storm was slamming the Midwest with heavy snow, so flying at any point was uncertain.

Aaron dialed Anna again. This time she answered.

"I have bad news," he said when he heard her voice. "Mom asked to see us this morning, but by the time I got to her bed she was already out again. Dr. Amer thinks she doesn't have long."

Anna was silent, but then Aaron heard her crying.

"Do you think you and Garrett can come back to the hospital now?"

"I don't believe this," Anna said.

"I know, I can't even think anymore. Everything feels surreal."

"This is crazy," Anna said. "The adoption agency just called and woke us up. The birth mom has gone into labor early and the baby is coming—today."

"What? Today?"

"Yeah. Today."

"Are you serious? When? Where?"

"That's the crazy part. The baby is being born at St. Luke's!" she said.

Anna arrived at the hospital a little over an hour later, and by noon a small group of close family had gathered in the ICU waiting room.

Aaron and Anna spent the afternoon and Christmas Eve by their mother's bedside. And, every hour or so, Anna and Garrett made the long walk to the maternity wing of St. Luke's to check on the arrival of their baby.

"Why does everything always happen at once?" Anna asked Aaron as they sat next to their mom, listening to the steady flow of oxygen and the sound of their mom's labored breath. "It's been five years of ups and downs. We lose dad, mom gets sick, the agency puts us on the waiting list—so many disappointments . . . and now our little girl is being born right down the hallway."

"I know," Aaron shook his head. "But it's finally happening. You're going to be a mother."

Anna returned his smile. "I wish mom could meet her."

"Me too," Aaron paused. "I know she'd love her so much."

Tears streaked down Anna's face. "I can't decide if I'm happy or sad. How can I celebrate when mom is dying?"

Aaron rose from his chair and gave Anna a hug, both of their faces stained with tears.

"Mom would want you to celebrate," Aaron said. "She would be bouncing off the walls if she could."

Anna wiped her face and took a deep breath. "I know."

"Come on. Go check on your baby, and I'll go tell everyone in the waiting room what's going on."

Well into the night, just a few hours before sunrise on Christmas morning, mom quietly slipped away to heaven.

After a few minutes of just sitting quietly beside her lifeless body, Aaron stepped out of her room and called Matt, his voice breaking as he explained that she was gone. They wept on the phone, sharing tears of sadness and relief.

"Mom's home," Matt managed.

"Yeah," Aaron struggled. "Home—and healed."

Coming face-to-face with death on Christmas morning was almost unbearable. Waves of emotion had rocked Aaron back and forth, but those words settled him like an anchor in a storm. He knew his mom was gone, but he also knew she was living on. Her fight was over. Her weary body was finally at rest.

———————

Aaron walked down to the NICU and found Anna and Garrett in a private room. He slowly opened the door and Anna waved for him to come in.

"Look how beautiful she is," Anna whispered.

"She's perfect," Garrett added.

"Is she okay? I mean, she's healthy and she's okay?" Aaron said, searching for the right way to ask.

Anna and Garrett both nodded.

"She's healthy," Anna said. "The doctor said she'll have to stay here for a few weeks as they wean her off of the drugs she's become accustomed to in the womb. But they think she's going to be okay."

Aaron leaned in closer to the incubator.

"She's beautiful," he stammered. "Just perfect. And she's *here*." He looked up to Anna and Garrett. "You guys have waited forever, but she's finally here."

"We already have a name picked out," Anna said. "We are naming her after mom."

Aaron stood up and let the news sink in. For a moment, the emotion was too much. He leaned back down, as close as he could to her face.

"Hi Grace. I'm your uncle Aaron. I love you so much." He wiped the tears from his face. "You are our little Christmas Grace."

There was a quiet knock at the door. Anna and Garrett's pastor, Jake, and his wife, Siena, stuck their heads into the room.

"Can we come in?" Siena whispered.

Anna smiled and motioned for them to come in.

As they entered the room they saw the tears on Aaron's face.

"Is something wrong?" Jake asked. "Is she all right?"

"She's amazing," Aaron managed through the tears. "We're naming her after mom."

"That's beautiful," Siena said.

"Can you believe she was born on Christmas morning?" Aaron said.

"If it's okay, we'd like to pray a dedication over her," Siena said.

After a minute or two, they gathered around Grace's little rolling incubator, and Siena's soft voice filled the room as she prayed for God's favor and thanked Him for the precious gift of Grace's life. As Siena was praying, Aaron reached into his pocket and pulled out the last note he had found by mom's bedside a week or so before.

She had known, somehow, that it would be her final words of encouragement before she was gone. When Siena finished, Aaron held the note out in the palm of his hand for them all to see:

See you soon. Love, Mom.

WAITING HERE FOR YOU

Published in Atlanta, Georgia by Passion Publishing

Cover and interior design by Leighton Ching and Faceout Studio

Imagery pages 28–29, 45, 60, 70-71 from Offset

Imagery page 50 from Shutterstock

Imagery page 78 © Andy Brophy, Terminus, 2013

Imagery page 86 from Stocksy

Clipart courtesy FCIT

ISBN-13: 978-0-9898-5082-7
Printed in Canada